COUNTING THE DAYS

Crazy Good Ideas for Long-Distance Relationships

D1569087

GREGG MICHAELSEN

**DISCLAIMER: As a male dating coach I am very good at what I do because of my years of studying the nuances of interpersonal relationships.
I have helped thousands of women understand men. That said, I am not a psychologist, doctor or licensed professional. So do not use my advice as a substitute if you need professional help.**

Women tell me how much I have helped them and I truly hope that I can HELP you too in your pursuit of that extraordinary man! I will provide you with powerful tools. YOU need to bring me your willingness to listen and CHANGE!

CONTENTS

As you are about to discover, communication is a very powerful tool and one of the most important skills you will require in your long-distance relationship.

To help you develop the best communication skills possible, I am offering you a FREE copy of my best-selling book, *The Power to Communicate*. The best thing about this book is that it's not just written for women, so you can share it with your partner and gain double the benefit!

To receive your free copy, simply go to
WhoHoldsTheCardsNow.com/counting-links

Introduction

Whether you find yourself in a long-distance relationship today or you are considering entering into one, there are some important things to know. Many people will try to discourage you by stating mythological statistics relating to long-distance relationships. Instead of basing the potential success or failure of your relationship on myths, why not get the facts and learn some valuable skills to ensure your relationship will withstand the test of time and distance?

Most recent statistics indicate that more than fourteen million people in the United States are in a long-distance relationship and that about fifty-eight percent of those are successful. You are not alone! Of those fourteen million people, between four and four and a half million of them are not married. Additionally, nearly four million married couples are in a long-distance relationship.

When looking at couples who are engaged, roughly seventy-five percent of them say their relationship was an LDR at some time or another and ten percent of married couples in the United States started out in an LDR.

Thirty-two and a half percent of those fourteen million people in long-distance relationships (LDRs) are college students. Less common, but still important are LDRs that occur due to one partner or the other being on active military duty. Yet another small percentage are away from one another for work-related reasons.

Unfortunately, roughly forty percent of LDRs will end in a breakup but seventy percent of those breakups occur due to unplanned changes. The average amount of time before an LDR breaks down completely is about four and a half months.

An LDR is defined as a relationship where partners live more than 125 miles apart. This means that for some relationships, a two to three-hour drive is all that is required to spend time together. This can be good news or bad news, depending on the expectations you've set for the relationship.

In the coming chapters, you'll learn some of the pitfalls to avoid in your LDR and some of the bonuses of being in an LDR, but most importantly, you'll discover dozens of ways in which you and your partner can avoid becoming one of the failed relationship statistics!

The truth is that there are many things you can both do to ensure relationship success and that's the focus of this book! In the coming chapters, you'll find:

- How to set 'rules' for your relationship
- How to have long-distance date nights
- How much communication is too much, and best practices for communicating
- How to create sexual tension
- How to enjoy your time apart
- Knowing if and when it's coming to an end
- Much. Much. More!

Your relationship is not doomed, simply because you and your partner have chosen to live apart for a while. Many LDRs are very strong, a result of actively working on building a strong relationship, just like you would if you lived in the same town.

1

Communication and the LDR

Without great communication, any relationship will struggle. This is true of your relationship with your boss, your family, your friends, and your partner, whether they live two or two hundred miles away. Solid communication is the backbone of every successful relationship.

What's In it for Them?

For the most part, society today maintains a *what's in it for me* attitude. When people think about a given situation, they first think about how the situation can benefit themselves. In order to have effective communication, however, it's important to view things from a *what's in it for them* (meaning the other person) perspective instead.

Let me share a personal example with you. I played hockey as a kid and I needed new skates, so I went to my mom with something that sounded like this, "MOM! I need new skates! Let's go get them!"

Well, I probably don't need to tell you that my approach didn't work. As kids will do, I got frustrated and yelled a little louder, hoping this would motivate her, but she was unfazed. I played a few more games in skates that were too small and hurt my feet.

This isn't just something kids do, it's something we all do. You know *what* you want, and you know you want it *now*. You want the short-term gratification of getting it now. It's often difficult to imagine that the person with whom you're trying to interact might have their own agenda. *Who knew!?*

If I had gone to my mom with this approach instead, I probably would have gotten my skates much sooner than I did, "Mom, I know you're really busy right now, but if I help out around the house with chores this weekend, do you think I could get some new hockey skates?"

This approach acknowledges that she's busy and my offer to help her shows that I'm not being selfish in my request, as in the earlier example—a demand for skates. When you acknowledge where the other person is and any challenges they might be facing, you disarm their automatic "No" response.

Let's look at this from another perspective.

Imagine you live in Ohio and you want to come visit me. You ask me for directions. *Suspend for the moment your knowledge of mobile apps that give directions.* I live in Boston, so when I provide the directions, I might say something as simple as, "When you get to my street, turn right and look for this address. It'll be on your right."

These directions assume that you're where I am, instead of where you are. I didn't take into account that you must drive through Ohio, Pennsylvania and a couple other states before you encounter my street. I began where I was, not where you were.

What is Their Truth?

Much like only being interested in your own point of view, it's easy to look at things through your truth, instead of someone else's. What does this mean?

Sometimes, when someone asks you to do something, their instructions might seem to be clear when, in fact, they're pretty muddy. Again, let's look at an example.

> *John and Annie have an LDR and are planning to spend a three-day weekend together next week. John sends Annie a text, "Hey Babe, I need to bring my dark blue suit back with me when I return. Can you make sure it's ready?"*

Now, this might seem clear, but what does *ready* mean? Ready could mean get it out and slide it into a protective covering. Ready could also mean there's a missing button, can you fix it, or it could mean would you take it to the dry cleaners for me.

Annie's best response is, *"Sure John, but let me be sure I understand. Would you like me to have it dry cleaned for you or do you just need me to get it out, so you don't forget it?"* Annie has restated John's request in a way that allows him to clarify what he needs from her. Now, John can reply with whichever of those scenarios he needs.

These types of misinterpretations happen frequently and without clarification, things can take an ugly turn. To Annie, John's request might have meant *just get it out* because if she were asking, that's what she would want, but by clarifying, she avoided John not having his suit ready when he returned home.

We tend to look at interactions with others through our own lenses, instead of theirs. It's natural and instinctive, but it's fixable. If you train yourself to restate important requests for clarification, you avoid applying your own truth instead of that of your partner.

Let's look at another quick example.

> *Brent and Tiff met online. Brent lives about two hours away from Tiff, but they hit it off and Brent asked Tiff to be in an LDR with him. Tiff's father was in the military and her parents got divorced, so her experience with LDRs is that they don't work. Brent's parents weren't apart for more than a couple of days, so he has no personal experience with it and is willing to give it a try. If Tiff replies, simply based on her own truth, she will decline, but if she sees the situation from Brent's perspective, she may indeed try it.*

When you try to force your truth on someone else, it will almost always end in conflict. You see the world one way; they see the world another and you both feel you're right. Instead, try to see the world through the eyes of the person with whom you're interacting. Try to see things from another point of view.

Stay Present in Your Conversations

Whether you're chatting with your significant other via Face-Time, on the phone or by text, stay present in the conversation. It's *so* easy to slip into thoughts such as:

- *He thinks he had a bad day; he doesn't know the half of what I went through today.*
- *I wonder if I remembered to turn off the coffee pot at work today.*
- *Should I go to the mall this weekend to get those pumps before the sale ends?*

Meanwhile, you've been asked an important question and you don't know how to respond without asking him to repeat that question, outing you as not paying attention.

This is really about developing great listening skills. Listening means actively paying attention to what the other person is saying, *without* trying to come up with a story to top theirs, allowing your thoughts to wander or just zoning out. You might *hear* what the other person is saying, but that doesn't mean you took it in, or that you can respond intelligently and empathetically.

Having good listening skills requires concentration and focus. It involves being mindfully aware of the conversation and the person speaking. To be a good listener, you should also wait a few seconds before formulating your response, rather than attempting to formulate it before the person speaking is even finished.

Great listening skills require you to avoid interrupting the person who is speaking. This is a toughie for many people and something we all slip into from time to time. Before you reply, consider whether what you're about to say adds anything positive and productive to the conversation. If someone is truly seeking your opinion, try to deliver it in the context of what was just said. Put yourself in the speaker's place and imagine the situation from their point of view.

The great thing about letting someone know you're listening is that they'll usually talk for less time. It's also important to know that people who have a habit of interrupting often are signaling low confidence. They're trying to interject to prove their worth—to you and to themselves.

Carefully Manage Oppositional Conversations

There are probably topics like *which team will win the Superbowl* and *who you plan to vote for in the next election* that might need to go untouched if you and your partner are on opposing sides. This may take some time to weed out.

When you are on opposite sides of a conversation, it doesn't mean you *can't* discuss it, but it does mean you need to discuss it respectfully and in a way that won't end in a fight. That opposition tone can be very difficult to avoid if you have a personal or professional stake in the outcome of the discussion.

It's one thing to playfully argue about whether butter pecan or chocolate chip cookie dough ice cream is the best flavor ever. It's a whole other thing to end up shouting at one another over Democrat versus Republican.

When you are discussing a topic that you know will strike opposition, recognize a few things:

- To listen to and acknowledge someone else's point of view does not mean you give up on what you believe in
- Acting rationally in a conversation shows impartiality—it says that you're mature enough to at least *see* the other person's point of view and acknowledge it; you don't need to agree with it, just acknowledge that it exists
- Just because you are reacting in a rational manner doesn't mean the person with whom you're speaking will return the favor, although keeping a cool head will help diffuse the situation, should it escalate
- When you allow someone to react to the conversation in their own way, you're telling them that you set aside any judgment

Be Understanding

This all boils down to one thing—being understanding. Conversation is about opening your mind to another point of view. It's about being an active listener who doesn't interrupt and waits to determine whether the response they have is helpful or harmful and moving forward from there.

Since most of your conversations with your LDR partner will be via text or email, you will need to be especially careful to use words that don't accidentally cause a problem. There is no way to interpret tone of voice in a text or email and something you might say jokingly can be mistaken easily.

Ask yourself these questions:

- Do I truly understand their point of view?
- Am I seeing this from my truth or theirs?
- Am I actively listening or am I zoned out/trying to best them?
- Do the solutions I'm about to offer provide positive impact?
- Am I building him up or tearing him down?
- Does he realize that I understand him?

2

Solving the Intimacy Problem

The most common problem in LDRs is intimacy. And let's be clear, right off, sex is not intimacy. You can have sex with someone and have zero intimacy—think hook-ups. Intimacy is built through time together, so it makes perfect sense that it can be more challenging in an LDR.

Be Sensitive to One Another's Needs

Your time together may be short—just two or three days. It's easy to try and over-plan that time together. You have so much to catch up on, so many things you want to do, friends and family who want to see your MIA partner.

And yet, your partner may need to accomplish a few things while he's home. He may need to run some errands or maybe he has chores he wants to do. He might need some down-time from a stressful week or time to unwind and not think about anything for a little while.

Men manage stress and emotional situations differently than you do. For him, time alone to lick his wounds or sort through his emotions is crucial in being able to move forward. If you've detected some stress in his week, allow him some time when he gets into town to just *be*. Ask him if he would like that alone time, instead of assuming he's ready to hit the ground running.

If you give him a little bit of time to process whatever he's got going on first, he will be present for the remainder of your time together. While he's doing that, go do your thing—whatever it is. Go grocery shopping, find a friend and have coffee together or do a workout, take a hot bath or read a book. Don't nag at him; wait until he emerges refreshed.

At the same time, if you've got something emotional going on, try to process it before you're together. He can't handle your highly emotional states because he isn't wired to experience them. Try to unload whatever stress and anxiety you're feeling before you meet. If you're the one traveling, use that time to meditate, listen to your favorite music or just rest. By the time you two are together, you will feel refreshed and ready to go.

Don't Let Problems Simmer

Problems that aren't addressed can be the demise of any relationship, but this can be especially true of an LDR. When something comes up, use those communication skills to work through it. Don't save it for when you're together.

Saving it causes a few negatives. First of all, the problem festers and gets bigger and uglier than it could be if managed earlier. If there are hurt feelings, anxiety will cause those feelings to grow as more and more doubt creeps in.

Saving a problem also forces the two of you to start your time together in disagreement or in a problem-solving mode. This can set the tone for your entire time together and then any chance of great communication and intimacy could be lost before you even get started.

Many people say they want to discuss problems in person, but this is simply a stall tactic. In an LDR couples can't play this game. When your relationship is long-distance, you must learn to communicate and unravel these problems as soon as they creep up.

Don't Imagine You're a Mind-Reader

It's so easy to allow your mind to wander when you're apart. You think you can read his mind and know what he's thinking. This causes you to create your own series of thoughts, based on your assumptions and before your partner knows it, you're mad at him and he has no clue as to why.

Instead of assuming what he thinks, ask him. Again, this boils down to solid communication, which is why it was the first chapter. Anxiety is when you allow your thoughts to move into future scenarios, playing them out in the most negative way you can imagine.

Instead, recognize that your anxiety is getting the best of you and stop this thought train. You can do it! Realize that your partner hasn't actually said or done anything you're imagining. Stop yourself from projecting a future that isn't real.

Amy and Rick live 150 miles apart. For the past three nights, Amy hasn't been able to reach Rick by phone. One night was fine, but three nights has Amy's mind going in all sorts of places. He's having an affair. He's dead in his bed and nobody has found him yet. He decided to break up with her, but he isn't going to tell her until he comes back.

The truth is that Rick has been working overtime so he could visit Amy this weekend. In order to completely focus, he's turned his phone on silent and set it aside. By the time he sees that Amy has called repeatedly, it's too late to call her back. Then, he gets up the next morning and starts early again.

Meanwhile, Amy has worried her way through several scenarios, none of which are good and by the time he gets into town, she's an emotional train wreck. They meet and she immediately falls to pieces. Rick is stymied and clueless.

After some discussion, Amy realizes that her anxiety was working against her, but Rick learns a valuable lesson too. He needs to at least text Amy, even if it's late, to tell her he's okay and he loves her. Men aren't big communicators, and he didn't realize it was as big a deal as it was to her.

Avoid *Too Much* Conversation

When you're apart and missing one another, especially early in the relationship, it's easy to want to spend hours talking on Facetime or Skype or whatever. Try to avoid this most of the time. The problem you will have is that when you're together, you won't have anything to share.

When you're spending this much time talking, you're neglecting things at home. Spending six hours in an evening talking to your beau means you're not out doing yoga, hanging with your friends or tending to hobbies.

Most men dislike small talk. They may engage in it at the beginning of a relationship, but that's because they feel they should. After they become more comfortable in the relationship, they'll drop it because it isn't natural.

Instead, use some level of radio silence. What I mean by this is that instead of texting non-stop throughout the day, send a "Good Morning" text and then let it go. Unless something truly important comes up, let the day pass without constant back and forth. I recommend this for all couples, not just long-distance couples.

When you do this, it makes your conversations later more meaningful. It doesn't mean those later discussions need to be hours long, it just means you can share something great about your day and he can do the same.

By limiting the amount of time you talk when you're apart, you're still tending to your life outside the relationship while maintaining a healthy level of communication. He can do things where he is with friends and coworkers and you can do the same.

This will keep him excited to hear from you when you do talk and you (and he) will have some fun stories to share!

Learn How Men Text

To say that men and women text differently would be a gross understatement. Here are just a few examples:

- Women text back and forth, with immediate responses; men do not
- Women text lines and lines of words; men do not and will ignore these
- Women pour out their emotions and vengeance through text; men ignore these

When you text a man, you can expect to wait at least twenty to thirty minutes, *at best*, before he replies. Anything sooner is a bonus. Most of the time, you may wait a couple of hours. Add time to this if it's during his workday or night. Some jobs prohibit phone time while others just frown upon it. If he has a closed office, he'll be better able to reply, but that's only if he isn't busy working.

Meanwhile, he's busy and not replying and you're getting angry. The longer he goes without answering, the worse your anxiety becomes, just like Amy in the example above.

Needing a reply immediately is a sign of neediness and low confidence. It sends a very negative signal to your partner. Once you send a text, try to busy yourself, instead of sitting there, staring at your phone. Read a book. Take a hot bath. Go for a run. Do *something* to take your mind off waiting for a reply.

Strive for independence during your LDR downtime.

Avoid Drifting Apart

It's so easy to build your own new experiences while you're away from one another, and the same for him. If you're not careful, you can grow apart through personal growth.

There are several things you can do to try and minimize the effect of personal growth. The first is to agree that you'll close the physical distance gap between you in a given period of time. Many things keep couples apart, including college or other forms of study, being in the military and work. Sometimes, as in the case of the military, it's more challenging to shorten the time and you must resolve to maintain closeness.

In other situations, one or the other of you may be able to move closer. It will require some work, like finding a new job and maybe a place to stay, but if your relationship is worth it, these are small sacrifices to make. It's always possible to move back "home" later if you are both agreeable.

Another way to avoid drifting apart is to plan frequent visits, taking turns traveling. Of course, the distance required will play a role in this, but try to be with one another as often as you can. This enables you to grow together and share experiences. If he tried rock climbing and loved it, the next time you're together, you can try it with him. Now, you've both grown and shared something, building intimacy as well.

Men like growing with you more than you think and it's a great way to stay close. Agree to include each other in new experiences, even if you've tried it on your own first. LDRs can fall apart because one partner took on a new adventure, new friends, and a new way of life while the other partner feels left out. Suddenly, they start to drift apart. Don't let this happen to your LDR!

Later in this book, you'll learn about some great long-distance date ideas you can share. These will help you reconnect and enjoy one another when you can't be together.

Inject Mystery

Nothing beats a surprise, and a surprise visit from you might be just what your relationship needs to keep things on track. This type of surprise is an excellent way to be mysterious, which is something you need in your relationship anyway.

There are other ways to insert mystery into your relationship. For example, send him a hand-written note, telling how excited you are to see him next time. Remind him of a wonderful experience you shared together and pique his senses.

Josh,

It's late and I was just sitting here thinking about that trip we took to Vermont last winter to go skiing. I was chuckling to myself over how many times I fell before I got the hang of it. It was great to feel your arms wrapping around me, scooping me out of the snow.

I can't wait to see you next weekend! Let's plan something great!

Amanda

This is a great way to stir some memories and remind him of intimacy you've built together in the past. It's short but lets him know in a nice way that you're thinking of him.

You can also send him a surprise gift. It doesn't need to be anything fancy and can even be something homemade like cookies or a favorite movie. You can even send him stuff to have a long-distance date night together. More on that later!

Anything you can do to keep him guessing is great! This keeps him from becoming bored and helps him anticipate your time together as much as you do.

Go Somewhere Else Together

While most of your visits will be him coming to you or you going to him, it might be fun to meet somewhere away from both homes. Exploring new places together is a great way to build intimacy. Those shared memories of wandering through the woods holding hands, hiking through the mountains or exploring the city block of a small town are priceless. Even a couple of days spent somewhere together injects plenty of intimacy.

Meeting away from either residence has its advantages. You will have fewer interruptions and both of you will feel like you are on vacation even if it's only for the weekend.

Sit down together with a calendar and plan out a few of these mini vacations throughout the year. You won't get bored doing the same old thing every weekend and you'll both be able to get away and decompress from the weekly grind.

Meet One Another's "Away" Friends

You both develop relationships in the places you live. You make friends everywhere—at work, at the gym, at the coffee shop and even on regular walks around your neighborhood. When you're together, try to become part of one another's "away" circles. Meet his friends where he lives and get to know them.

When he comes to visit, include your friends in some of your plans so he can get to know them. By meeting one another's friends, you not only broaden your circle, but you get deeper involved in one another's lives. This can lead to shared experiences with friends, like weekend getaways, social gatherings and so on. Be sure to follow these new friends on social media too. This will help you have some idea of the upcoming events in your partner's life—not so you can become jealous, but so you can plan to be involved or ask about it when you talk.

When you're apart, you can feel isolated, but by having these new friends to share with and talk to, you'll be less likely to feel this way. You'll get a better idea of how your partner spends his free time and will feel more involved, if only from a distance.

Finally, by knowing each other's friends, you build trust. You know who he is with and he knows who you are with.

Never Stop Flirting

This is a staple in any relationship. Never stop flirting with your partner, regardless of how long you've been together. Not only does this spice things up, but it reminds you both of how attracted you are to each other.

Flirting can be done by text or when you're talking on the phone and definitely when you're together. Wear that something slinky he loves and send him a photo. Be sure to make sure he knows how much you appreciate him and that you're thankful to have him in your life.

Gratitude is one of the best predictors of a successful relationship. Being grateful for your partner's qualities helps you focus on the good instead of dwelling on the bad. Appreciation goes a long way in making your guy feel that the effort he's putting in is worth it. Everyone likes to be appreciated!

Know His Love Language

Even from a distance, you can use his love language to keep the intimacy alive. Gary Chapman's Five Love Languages help couples learn how to show love to one another in a way that they like to receive it. For example, if your partner's love language is receiving gifts, you can show him how much you love him by sending that letter above or a box of his favorite cookies.

There are quizzes online to help you determine what your love language is, and you can both take them. If you don't want to do that, pay attention to how he shows his love to you. If he touches you frequently with gentle massaging or holding your hand, chances are his love language is physical touch. If he is always telling you how much he appreciates the little things you do, it's probably words of affirmation.

Share a Little More

Earlier I said not to text one another all day, and I stand by that, but also, when you do talk, be sure to share the details of what's going on in your life. Ask him questions about his life as well. If you were together, at the end of a workday, you would probably share certain things. By doing so, even long-distance, you're keeping that same level of involvement in each other's lives.

This helps you to be sympathetic to one another's needs and also allows you to empathize with each other. You will gain a deeper understanding of each other and will be able to better plan your time together.

Have Shared Goals

It's important to have personal goals, but it can really draw you closer to one another if you have relationship goals too. These goals don't all need to be serious, "Save $3000 for a vacation" types of goals. They can be goals focused on your time together.

Other goals can be more long-term, like setting a goal for when you will live in the same town or saving up for that big vacation together. Smaller goals can focus on enjoying different types of weekends together. One might be a Netflix binge weekend while another could be exploring a nearby town. These help you have something to look forward to and work toward together.

3

The "Rules" of Long-Distance Relationships

RULE #1: Set Reasonable Expectations

You both need to be clear about what your expectations are in a long-distance relationship. This doesn't mean that if you've just met, you need to set a marriage expectation. That's not what I mean. What this means is deciding how often you'll be together and who travels when.

Expectations about how often you'll enjoy a virtual date night or just chat on the phone help keep tempers from flaring. Are you both still allowed to date other people? Early in a relationship, this is an okay thing to do.

Once these expectations are in place, remind yourself of them when you start feeling left out or jealous. This is your low confidence and anxiety trying to creep in and mess things up. Don't listen to either one!

RULE #2: This is an Opportunity!

Language is everything! The way you frame any situation determines how you view it. If you frame a long-distance relationship as problematic, it will be, but if you frame it as an opportunity, it'll feel more positive.

There is a Chinese proverb that kinda-sorta fits here. *Real gold does not fear the test of fire.* What it really means is that a person of integrity can withstand any test, so it kind of fits. Integrity is defined as honest with strong moral principles, so this fits in a relationship too. If your relationship can withstand the test of distance, and you work at it, it can withstand anything.

If you both truly believe that this relationship will become stronger with the distance between you, it will happen.

RULE #3: Communication is NOT Optional

I hate to keep pounding home the same point, but you must have great communication if you want this relationship to succeed. This means not hiding things from one another or making assumptions based on anxiety or jealousy.

Try to keep your communication creative. Instead of just a text every morning to say, "Good Morning", try sending a little video of you wishing him a great day or send him a sexy "Good Night Sweetheart" message before bed.

Remember, don't make morning and evening communication mandatory or you will just be let down. Stay flexible.

You can also use images or those great little gif animations on your phone to send him messages. The point is to change things up and keep the intrigue alive. The same old "Good Morning" message every day becomes so regular that you don't even recognize it, but if you're waiting to see what *kind* of good morning message you get, that's a whole other story!

RULE #4: Try to Maintain a Schedule

There is something to be said for predictability when you're in an LDR. You and your partner both know when the other is busy working out or running errands and you avoid expecting a phone call during that time.

Also, it helps you plan your time together. If you know he does his big workout of the week on Saturday morning, you can either plan to arrive after he's done or schedule something for yourself during that time.

As part of this regular schedule, don't forget to schedule that all-important date night as well as regular times to talk. These connections are invaluable to you when you're apart. If you decide you need to break from the routine and it will impact communication with your partner, let him know and reschedule a time to connect.

Maintaining a schedule does not mean the schedule cannot change. It might, often, and that's a good thing.

RULE #5: Stay Out of Risky Situations

Avoid unnecessary drama by avoiding situations which could get you into trouble or cause your partner to feel a little anxious. This means if your ex is going to be at a party, it's probably best to sit it out. If you're out with your girlfriends, don't get so drunk that you make poor choices.

Also watch what you do that could be posted on social media. Pictures can easily be misunderstood, and drama can escalate before you've had a chance to explain, if there is a valid explanation.

Trust is crucial to your relationship success—to any relationship success. Building trust means showing your partner that when you're apart, you can be trusted, and vice versa.

RULE #6: Don't Listen to Naysayers

If someone has tried an LDR and failed, they will be the first to tell you that *all* LDRs fail. Don't listen to this nonsense. People tend to insert their own experiences as if they're the gospel truth. Your situation is different, and you need to remember that.

Even *if* she starts talking about how "similar" the relationships are, the truth is they aren't for one good reason. You and your partner are not your friend and her ex. You haven't gone about it in the same way. You may have different expectations and most importantly, you're reading this book to make sure your relationship succeeds.

The statistics cited at the beginning of this book should help you to recognize that you have a great chance of success if you do things right. Kindly tell your friend thanks for the words of advice and then try to hang out with her less. You need positive people in your life!

RULE #7: Don't Read into Things More than is There

Your guy sent you what seems like a wonderful email, but there is one sentence in it that has you concerned. Here's the thing about email and texting—you can't see his face when he says those words. You can't see if he's smiling or frowning. You can't tell if he's trying to be playful or if he's seriously got an issue with something.

Let it go!

I have done this unintentionally! I send a text, like I would to a male friend, thinking it's perfectly harmless to my girlfriend and BAM! What I texted did not convey the right meaning because I left out a word.

If you have a concern about something he says in a text or email, *ask him*, instead of allowing your anxiety to run amok. It's when you start making assumptions that trouble begins. Instead of doing that, just ask. If your relationship isn't on solid enough ground for you to ask about a comment he made in a text or email, you need to think about shoring it up. Don't be afraid to ask.

RULE #8: Stay Positive

It's important to maintain a positive outlook on your relationship and your life in general. Negativity bogs you down and allows your anxious thoughts to take over. When a friend suggests that your guy may be fooling around on you, dismiss it. Chances are, she's just jealous that you've got something great and she's still looking.

Additionally, the positive attitude helps him stay positive. If you call and you're all Debbie Downer, by the time your call is over, you'll both be down in the dumps. This relationship has challenges, but you knew that going in. Instead of focusing on those challenges, focus on the great things you can do together, whether virtually or in person. Build positive memories and focus on those. Allow the relationship to be the vessel to build you both up after a crappy week!

When negativity begins, look for the positive of the situation. Maybe the two of you had an argument the last time you were together. Was there great make-up sex after? Did you both laugh about how ridiculous the argument was? What was the good? What you can do better? Focus on *that*, instead of the negative.

RULE #9: Try to Limit Screen Time

When you're on a virtual date or together in person, try to limit your screen time so you can focus on one another. Of course, there will be the call from mom to make sure you arrived intact but try not to spend two hours on the phone with your best friend, talking her down off a ledge because her boyfriend didn't say hello the same way this morning as he did last week.

Your time together is precious, and you should treat it that way by focusing your energy on your partner. You'll have lots of time when you and your guy are apart to help your friend.

RULE #10: Establish Boundaries

You should have boundaries, regardless of the distance between you and your partner. Those boundaries should apply to everyone in your life, not just your significant other. Still, when it comes to enjoying a long-distance relationship, there may be a few other boundaries to set.

Decide what's best for you both when it comes to how often to text, talk by phone, or video chat. What is a visitation schedule that works best for both of you? If you're not married, do you stay together when visiting or is there an alternate location for the visitor? What about kids? All of these things need to be worked through.

These boundaries are about addressing the needs both of you have and coming to some sort of compromise. If you feel you need a text every day, but he would rather text every two or three days, find the middle ground that works for both of you. Then, don't get all worked up when you don't hear from him on the schedule you *want* versus the schedule you agreed on.

4

Long Distance Date Nights

Since you aren't together all the time, it's really important to schedule regular date nights. This helps you continue to connect on an emotional level, even with the distance. How can you have long distance date nights? I thought you'd never ask!

Enjoy a Movie Night

The easiest date night activity you can find is to enjoy a movie night together. If you've both got access to Netflix, try the Netflix Party app. You can stop and start the movie on multiple screens so that if someone needs a bathroom break or more popcorn, you won't miss anything! Share your thoughts and comments, just like you would in person and enjoy this time together. This is a great way to binge watch something you both enjoy too.

Amazon Prime has also released a similar feature when you're watching a movie on their site or app.

Have a Virtual Dinner Date

I alluded to this earlier. If you think your guy won't have the supplies, mail him a dinner kit that includes candles, matches and maybe even a nice tablecloth. You prepare the same at your home, then order takeout for the two of you. You can even have a bottle of his favorite beer or wine sent over with today's delivery systems. Then, all you need to do is call each other on FaceTime or another app and enjoy your dinner together.

Dance Together—Sorta

If you love to dance, put on some music and dance—you at your place, him at his. Sing along if you'd like and really enjoy the time. Imagine you're out at a club. Dance, then take breaks and sit down to enjoy a drink or conversation. Treat this just like an evening out, except you're home! Try to stay sober, though. Stay focused on the time together, not on getting trashed.

Vacation in a Box

If you can't be together to take a vacation right now, why not prepare a vacation in a box? Where would you like to go? Hawaii? Gather some leis, sunglasses, tropical drink mix and even some of those cute little drink umbrellas. Send him a box containing all the goodies he needs to enjoy the vacation on his end while you do the same at home. Spend plenty of time on Facetime or Skype sipping your drinks and hula dancing. You may even be able to find some virtual tours on the islands that you can do together.

This is a great way to "get away from it all" while being apart. Sure, it's not really sandy beaches, but you can take the real vacation when you're together sometime. For now, enjoy what you have.

Book Club

If you're both avid readers, why not read a book together? Once a week, you can talk about the book together and share thoughts. This is an awesome way to get to know one another a little deeper while doing something you both love. The bonus is that you can do your reading while you're not talking, thus filling up some of that empty time!

Have a Couple's Journal

Sharing a couple's journal like this great one helps you both connect on a variety of levels. You can share both your schedules, write answers to prompts and share experiences together. These journals are a great way to mark your time together and apart.

Grab a copy of *Me. You. Together Forever* for 25%
with this special, reader-only link:
https://who-holds-the-cards-now.myshopify.com/products/
me-you-together-forever-printable-couples-journal-25-off

A cousin to the couple's journal is a bucket list journal, like this, which you can also get for 25% off with a special, reader-only link. Decide what your couple's bucket list includes and then plan to tick those bucket list items off. Take pictures and write about the experiences so you'll have memories for years to come.

Learn a New Skill "Together"

There are tons of classes you can take online. Why not sign up for an online cooking class or a photography class and learn something new together? Sharing a hobby with your partner helps build intimacy and great memories. It gives you something you will always be able to enjoy together.

Enjoy an Evening Outdoors

If you both have nice weather, why not sit outside and stargaze? You may both see different things, but that just adds intrigue. If it's a little chilly, grab some hot cocoa or a brandy to warm you up and snuggle under a blanket while you share the sights and smells of the evening.

If you can and it's safe, take a walk around and enjoy the sights, sharing again what you see. This is a great way to get to know the area your partner lives in and appreciate where you are.

Have an "Unboxing" Date

Nothing is more exciting than receiving a box in the mail. Why not agree to send one another boxes to open on your next date night? These boxes can be themed or just random stuff. Agree on a spending limit so nobody feels they've been slighted. Decide on a date night and then make sure you and your partner get your boxes mailed in time.

Once the date begins, you can both open your boxes to see what's inside. This builds excitement and also gives you the chance to do something special for one another. Your gifts can be fun, playful, sexy, useful or whatever. The idea is to put some heart into it and surprise your partner.

Pillow Talk

Those nights where you just lay in bed and talk don't need to be reserved for when you're together. You can still enjoy an evening of pillow talk by phone! I know it's not quite the same, but these times can still be very intimate and beautiful. Of course, how far you take that pillow talk is completely up to you, so snuggle up and get comfy.

The Sky is the Limit

With technology today, if you can do it in person, you can probably do it virtually. The possibilities for virtual date nights are only limited by your imagination! Get creative. Work off what you both enjoy or something you would both like to do, then make it happen. The point is to spend time together doing something fun.

5

Activities for Long-Distance Couples

It may surprise you to find out how many things couples can do from a distance. Try the activities on this list and see which ones you and your partner enjoy the most. Also note that if you make a daily routine out of an activity, it will give you a sense of normalcy and make you feel like more of a "real" couple.

- Write old-fashioned love letters or poems to each other
- Send funny or charming e-cards to each other
- Play multiplayer games online together
- Play Mad Libs online or over the phone
- Watch a television show or movie at the same time
- Read chapters of a book to each other
- Hang out in a virtual world such as Second Life
- Send baked goods or candy
- Solve a newspaper's crossword puzzle together
- Leave romantic or naughty voice mail messages for each other
- Make a collage or design a web page dedicated to your partner
- Make mix tapes or playlists for each other

- Send your partner pictures of yourself wearing provocative outfits in clothing store dressing rooms
- Play strip poker via webcam
- Make a reading list and have your own little book club
- Using the same recipe, try cooking something simultaneously
- Make drawings for each other... even if they're just stick figures
- Take an online quiz separately, and then compare the results
  Send a care package containing edible and nonedible items
- Find and send cheesy or tourist-y post cards to each other
- Write a poem together, one line at a time or one word at a time
- Send a recording of yourself singing, even if your voice is awful
- Leave unexpected love notes on each other's Facebook or Twitter accounts
- Use Google Maps to plot out a pretend vacation
- Send handmade art and crafts
- Send your partner a text message in code and see if he or she can decipher it

6

Creating Sexual Tension from a Distance

One of the biggest challenges in an LDR is keeping the sexual tension and desire alive.

Intimacy can fall off during the potentially long periods of being apart, and when intimacy falls off, the mice will sometimes play.

Your SO can't see you, so he can't become aroused by your presence, like he can when you are in close proximity, so you need to get creative and use technology to your advantage.

Here are a few great tips to keep the sexual tension alive.

Masturbate Together

Facetime works for this. There are also sex toys that you can remotely control that work great with your partner! We-Vibe is an excellent example. No longer do you have to be with your guy.

Can you imagine working all day knowing that you will be getting off with your partner, who lives 200 miles away, while having control over the process later??!! Oh Yeah!

Talk Dirty

Dirty talk is so under-utilized in relationships! People are afraid of being judged by their SO if they try this. *Nonsense.* Declare a no-judgement zone and start role playing. Threesomes, albino goats, whip cream and handcuffs are all in play! Once you get over the initial toe-dipping, talking dirty can be extremely exciting. Combine We-Vibe and dirty talk for an extra bonus!

Send Reminders of You Without You

Send pics of your panties and bra along with your vibe to him. Put a bottle of your perfume in the shot along with silk sheets. Maybe add your favorite pumps. The very image of your stuff will drive him crazy!

Audio Orgasm

Another great way to keep the sexual tension alive is an audio orgasm. Anyone can sext but that's giving away too much, in my opinion. Instead, record yourself masturbating into orgasm. The first time you can say what you are doing to get there. Later, just send the audio!

For another variation—send him a video in near darkness while you masturbate. Let him enjoy sneak peeks of you while he listens.

R-Rated Apps

Instead of just texting each other, there are apps available to take things to another level. Desire, for example, allows you to hand out and receive dares.

This is what the app claims: *Desire is a fun way to play with that special person in your life, your love! If you are dating, married or crazy in love, Desire keeps that sweet romance with your other half and adds even more spicy and fun to your relationship.*

InTheMood is another example of this kind of app.

If the two of you try even half of these ideas, your sex life will be 100 times better than most who are able to see each other every day. The difference is that you are working with unique communication tools because you must. I'm getting myself worked up just talking about this stuff!

7

How to Enjoy Your Time Apart

It's important to enjoy your time apart as much as you enjoy your time together. Sure, you have your job and that may or may not fall into the category of enjoyable, but your job only occupies so many hours of your week. How can you leverage the remaining time?

Of course, some of it is taken up talking to your beau or enjoying a virtual date night together, but that still leaves you with a bunch of time to fill. The trick is to fill it productively and in a way that keeps negativity out and positivity in.

It is important to enjoy your time apart as much as you enjoy your time together. Why? Because if you fill your life outside of your LDR with exciting adventures, passions, and hobbies, guess what?

You become happy, confident, and interesting!

Now, when you chat with your ex you have exciting stuff to share with him. He sees you as this independent woman who he should never let go. Your vibrant social life motivates him to do the same so you both grow as individuals inside and outside your relationship.

Do not underestimate how important your time apart becomes!

Have a Hobby

Hobbies are great for everyone. You learn a new skill and you have an activity to go to when you need something to do. A hobby shouldn't be something you dread doing but something that brings joy to your life.

If you don't already have a hobby, try some on for size. There are as many hobbies as there are people so I can't exactly provide you with a list, but I can make a couple of suggestions on how to figure it out.

The easiest thing is to ask friends what their hobbies are and ask them to give you a lesson. This way, someone who knows what they're doing can tell you what you truly do and don't need to have to get started. Another way is to prowl around YouTube. There are videos on *everything*. Watch some videos and get a feel for what's out there then gather a few supplies and try it on for size.

You can also ask family members what they're into. Maybe mom was always into painting or embroidery. Ask her for some ideas on what you can do to get started. My final suggestion is to go to a hobby store or a craft store and wander around. Many of them have sample projects sitting out and they sell the supplies to complete the projects.

Volunteer

Volunteer work is very rewarding, and you get to meet new people while working for a cause you believe in. Many types of places use volunteers to make their business run efficiently. In my town, the local theater organization uses volunteers for ushers, as do sports venues. Museums often have volunteers to provide tours or work gift shops.

Of course, if you're into animals, why not check out the local zoo, pet stores or shelters? Churches always need volunteers to help out with various projects, as do medical facilities. Another great place to volunteer is at senior homes but check on their rules for visitors before deciding to engage.

Stay Connected to Friends

Maintaining your friendships outside of your relationship is crucial to keeping busy while you're apart. Even if you and your partner lived together, this would be an important thing! Continue to enjoy the occasional girls' night, have lunches with your friends and do all the same things you did before you met your guy.

Having friendships outside of your relationship gives you a valuable resource. When you're feeling overly emotional, you can talk to those friends. When your guy wants to hang out with his friends, you can hang with yours. Don't ditch these connections, just because you found a guy.

Trust me, he will love you for this. Guys all want a sense of independence and that is why you keep you friends and hobbies alive.

As I say all the time, in all my books, *never make your guy your hobby or you will be toast!*

Maintain or Improve Your Physical Health

Many women take offense to this suggestion, but I don't say it to help you become more attractive to a man. I tell you this for your own good. Men and women alike don't often make time to take care of themselves. Work, kids, and other demands get in the way of doing the most important thing you can do—take care of you.

This not only means developing a workout routine but eating healthy and making time for self-care. Spend some quiet time reading or meditating. Enjoy a spa day, either at home or out somewhere. Sit back with some music you enjoy and a glass of wine and just relax. These things allow your body to take a break. Your mind can reset, and you can relax all over.

Nobody but you can take care of you, so you need to stay on top of it. Nothing would be worse than coming up on a weekend together, only to become ill and have to reschedule.

And guess what? When I see my girl taking care of herself, I see a high-value woman who knows her worth, and it motivates me to do the same to 'keep up' with her.

8

Is This the End?

The problem with a long-distance relationship is that too many things can be assumed too quickly. If your guy doesn't call when you think he should, you automatically assume it's because he's out with someone else. The truth may be that he was exhausted and fell asleep before it was time to call.

Still, there are signs that the relationship may be losing steam. This doesn't mean it has to be over, though, if you recognize it in time and feel it's worth reviving.

There's No Plan to Stay Together

This isn't a problem for everyone, but it may be a problem for you. You and your guy need to have some clear expectations about when the two of you will live together permanently. If you're both okay staying distant, fine, but many couples are not.

Have an honest discussion about this early in your relationship so you aren't so invested and more deeply hurt later. As you discuss the possibility of an LDR, talk about how long the distance may last and how the two of you will unite under one roof, or at least one zip code. If this is a temporary job assignment or a stint away because one of you is in the military, you know there is an end in sight. The same goes with college—there is a graduation date, but that doesn't ensure the distance will close.

Be honest about what you think you can tolerate and listen to his concerns and expectations. Can you come to an agreement on this? If not, it may be time to cut those strings.

One of You Drops Communication

When you're mentally done, you may stop texting him or vice versa. You've already begun to distance yourself by wanting to communicate less. If it's him, make sure there isn't another reason, like a big work project or illness that's keeping him from his normal schedule.

Communication when you're apart is all you have to stay connected. Dropping communication begins to cause the relationship to deteriorate. Assumptions and anxieties begin to develop, feelings get hurt and before you know it, everyone is irritated and wham—it's over.

If you notice this change, have an honest discussion about it. Do you just need to change the pace of your communication or is one of you truly done with things? The only way to find out is to talk about it.

Meeting Times Grow Farther Apart

Early in the relationship, you were so excited to see one another and you worked hard to get together once every few weeks. Now, it just isn't as important to you, or he isn't as anxious to schedule his trip to see you.

Instead of making plans to get together, you seem to be finding reasons *not* to visit. *"Gee Bill, I'd love to come next weekend, but I already made plans to see a Movie with Gina. Maybe in a couple of weeks, okay?"* But in a couple of weeks, neither of you are making plans.

In this case, it's important to schedule that time together to see if there's still a spark. If not, you can use that time together to have the dreaded goodbye talk.

The Passion is Gone

Early in a relationship, you have all kinds of passion, but as time passes, it can wear off. There's no real reason for this to happen unless you're truly no longer interested. Even from a distance, if you use some of the things you've read in this book, you should be able to keep things passionate.

When you're together, you should still feel that old spark and traveling to see one another should be something you look forward to with genuine excitement and anticipation. It's when that excitement and anticipation are gone that you should begin to wonder.

Nothing but Hot Buttons

Any relationship reaches its end when all you're doing is pushing one another's hot buttons. In a long-distance relationship, it's a glaring sign that something isn't working for one or both of you. At this point, you need to take a step back and examine exactly where this is coming from.

Are you frustrated about communication? Would you like to be together more often? Are there trust issues or is it just that you've gotten to know one another better and you don't like what you see?

If you can't work through the issues, it's time to let this one go.

You're the Only One Trying

You're sending little gifts that he should love. You're sticking to the communication schedule you both agreed upon. You're doing everything right, or so you think. Meanwhile, he's barely 'showing up' for the relationship. He may text, but it's dry and unemotional. Phone calls are painfully short and lack any sign of interest on his part.

When you find yourself in this spot, you can assume he's lost interest in the relationship and it may be time to let it go.

Your Gut Says it's Time

Something doesn't feel right. You're having trouble getting your feelings across. You question whether this relationship is going to last. Maybe it just feels like something is missing. A part of you wants everything to be okay, but the rest of you is saying, "It's over."

Sometimes, your mind just knows before the rest of you realizes what's happening. Eventually, it'll send you signals to let you know that you've got some thinking to do.

The Relationship is Taking its Toll on the Rest of Your Life

Sometimes, relationships become toxic for both of you. Instead of adding something to your life, it's taking away. You can't seem to achieve your goals because you spend so much time on Skype and texting. The travel is bogging you down and you feel like it's more of a burden than a blessing.

When the relationship feels like it's ruining your life instead of making it better, it's toxic to you and it's probably time to let it go. If this was the right relationship for you, things in your life would align around it better. You would figure out how to make those things all happen.

But you aren't, and that is because it's just not the right relationship for you.

9

Making Your Budget Work

If money is not an issue, then skip this chapter. But what I find from my thousands of readers is that money does stop many of them from getting together so I threw in this chapter.

There's no doubt about it, being in a long-distance relationship is a strain on the budget. Whether you need to drive to meet up or fly, there are expenses. If you meet in a neutral location, you also have the expense of a place to stay.

Saving on Flying

The easiest thing to do to save on flights is to sign up for frequent flyer or other memberships associated with accumulating points for discounts. Some airlines even have credit cards you can sign up for and earn points with.

You can also fly during off-peak times, like early in the morning or late at night. In today's world of technology, there's no reason to do anything but search the various websites to find the best deal. They'll often provide you with alternative fight times to help you save.

If the distance is far enough to fly but close enough to travel by road, why not take a bus or a train? Yes, it will take longer, but you can use your laptop or tablet and still get things done. Those trips are usually much less expensive than a flight.

Regardless of which mode of transportation you choose, try to pack light. It seems to vary from day to day whether airlines are charging for checked bags or not. If you're just going for the weekend, you should be able to get that into a carryon bag without too much trouble. Remember, you're not going to be part of a fashion runway show, you're going to spend time with your guy! He won't care if you bring one pair of shoes or ten.

Saving on Driving

There isn't a lot you can do to save if you're driving, but you can fill up your tank before you leave instead of on the road. Often, near-highway prices are higher for gasoline than those further from the main roads.

It may save you money on something else, like groceries, to purchase gift cards for the gas stations you'll encounter. Just make sure that the cards you buy at home are good along your route. Different states have different companies.

Additionally, getting an oil change and making sure your tires are properly inflated can save you some gas as you drive. Pack sandwiches, snacks, and beverages so you don't need to stop and buy food on the road. This will save you a great deal, depending on how long your trip is. Don't forget to keep your windows up. Having them down creates drag which uses more gas.

And finally, plan your trip. Make sure you know when and where you can stop for bathroom breaks or to gas up the car. Know how many miles you're traveling and what your route is. With the apps available today, there's no reason for a trip that has no planned route.

Planning Your Activities Together

It can be tempting to bring your guy a lavish gift, to let him know how much you care, but your trip could also be considered a gift, so if you want to bring him something, why not bake him his favorite cookies or bring the fixings for his favorite meal that you cook together?

Have a budget in mind for your trip. Know what you plan to spend on gasoline if you're driving, food, snacks, and entertainment. Are you planning to go to a movie? Is a friend having a party? Is this a special occasion when you'll be going out to eat?

Work together to make sure you don't break his bank or your own. The point is to spend time together and you don't need to spend a ton of money to do that. It might be more enjoyable to do a date night Netflix binge or play some date night games. You may find there are specific hours when museums or other venues offer discounted entries—sometimes free.

Work Together

There's no worse feeling than having someone come to visit when you're five bucks from broke. Maybe your car needed a ton of work during the past couple of weeks and you're strapped. Then, your partner shows up and wants to paint the town red. It's embarrassing to say, "Sorry Honey, I'm broke."

Instead, plan your trip ahead of time and together. It might be helpful to work off that bucket list you created together. Limit yourselves to one money activity and spend the rest of the time doing things that don't cost money. If you want to go out, go for a walk or a hike in the woods. Sit in the park and people watch or walk the downtown streets and window shop. There are always things to do for free.

What you don't want to do is expect your guy to pay for everything. Yes, you just paid to travel there, but he will pay to come visit you as well and you'll expect him to pay then too, right? Be prepared to help pay for things. If he offers to pay, fine, but your offer ensures him that you're not just there to strip his bank account.

10

Building a Foundation of Trust

It's very difficult to maintain an LDR if you have no trust. In fact, it's impossible. Trust is the cornerstone of any relationship, but in a long-distance relationship, it's crucial to survival. Why?

No Trust = Jealousy = Problems

When there is no trust, it's very easy to become jealous. When you're apart, you wonder if he's secretly dating that cute girl from accounting that you met at the party a few months ago. You thought for sure she flashed him a secret smile when she thought you weren't looking.

As the old saying goes, trust is earned, but I would like you to think about this for a moment. I believe trust is inherent with someone until it's broken. Maybe that's just my good-hearted nature, but I believe most people can be trusted until they prove to me that I'm wrong.

If you have difficulty trusting, it might not be because of something your partner has done, but an overriding trust issue you have with everyone. If this is the case, you'll need to work through that on your own.

If your partner has given you no good reason to believe he's cheating, it's best to leave those jealous thoughts behind. Until you have proof of something going on, you're better off to put those thoughts out of your mind. Something else is causing them, like that trust issue you have with everyone or a lack of confidence on your part—a belief that there's no real way a guy like him could be interested in a woman like you.

That's something you can work on! So is an overriding trust issue. Finding out he's a schmuck and really is cheating on you means bye-bye.

As many of you know I am a life coach first so I can help you with your confidence through my books, courses, and free stuff on my website.

How do You Build Trust in a Relationship?

The only thing you can control is the level of trust your partner has in you, assuming you don't have trust issues of your own or low confidence. How can you build trust with your partner?

Be Trustworthy

If you want someone to trust you, be trustworthy. It seems basic and simplistic, but it's true. If you say you will be available to talk to him at 7:00 on Tuesday evening, be available. If you say you're coming for a visit in two weeks, don't put it off another week unless you're physically ill.

Whatever you say you'll do, do it. Wherever you say you'll be, be there.

Expect the same from him!

Be Transparent

Secrets are best left for birthday and holiday gifts, not for couples. Don't suddenly block him from your social media accounts or decide you don't want to have a face-to-face call with him. Don't avoid talking to him about important issues.

These all lead people to believe you have secrets, whether you do or not. Be transparent. Live your life the way you always have. If you enjoy posting photos of time spent with your girlfriends, keep doing it, even if there's a cute guy in the photo. He was flirting with your friend, not you. Hiding things just leads to doubt and anxiety.

Tell the Truth

Don't lie to your partner, no matter how small the lie seems. Once someone figures out you've lied, they begin to wonder what else you may have lied about. It sprouts doubt, which takes root and grows like a giant sequoia.

I cannot emphasize this enough. Once you get caught in a lie a man starts to question everything!

Lies also include *not* saying things. A lie of omission is just as bad as telling something that's untrue. It has the same effect. If you *forgot* to mention your new coworker, who just happens to be drop-dead gorgeous, what else did you forget?

Confess Quickly When Needed

Sometimes, you break one of those rules. It might not have been intentional. Maybe you *did* forget to tell him about the cute work guy because you're not interested in him, but your guy finds out about him anyway and wonders why you didn't mention it.

You know when you've goofed and the quickest way to diffuse the situation is to own it and move on. If this puts a dent in his trust for you, you'll need to earn it back, but know that it won't happen overnight.

Allow Yourself to be Vulnerable

A person doesn't show his or her vulnerable side unless they trust that they won't get hurt doing so. Men are very slow to show their vulnerabilities because they're often raised to believe it's not manly. Once a man trusts you, he will show his vulnerable side, slowly.

When you show your soft underbelly to someone, you're telling them you trust them with this part of yourself. You've given them something special about you that they need to hold dear. When someone shares something that makes them feel vulnerable, they are showing you that they trust you to be careful with this piece of them.

Whatever you do, do *not* share something vulnerable about your partner to others. This is a huge breech of trust and it will be a very long time before he is vulnerable with you again, if ever.

Show Respect

Have you ever been with someone who treats others rudely, regardless of how they're being treated? Imagine the person who is always rude to wait staff at a restaurant or the person who just never has anything nice to say on social media.

When people are this negative, they've got some issues going on. There is a complete lack of self-respect, let alone respect for others. Their self-worth and confidence may also be pretty low and their way of feeling *bigger* is to make someone else feel small.

I read a story recently about a hotel front desk clerk who had a horribly negative interaction with a customer. This customer had made a mistake, and rather than own it, he had blamed it on the clerk. The clerk maintained a high level of respect and calm while dealing with the customer.

When the next customer stepped up, the clerk greeted him in a most friendly manner. The customer commented, "I commend you for how you handled that person just now. He was very disrespectful." The clerk replied, "Well, he had to unload his stuff on somebody, and I happened to be in the line of fire. I don't know what may have just happened to him or what he has going on, but I imagine that everyone is good underneath, somewhere."

Even though the customer was extremely disrespectful, the clerk maintained his level of respect for that man and the one after, thus earning him the respect of the second customer. The interaction could have gone completely different and he would have lost the respect of the second customer and anyone else around him.

Be Willing to Extend the Benefit of the Doubt

You probably give someone you've known for a long time the benefit of the doubt when a question arises, but if someone new raises concerns, you're less likely to be so gracious.

This is human nature, so you must work hard to extend that benefit of the doubt to someone new in your life. Let him come through for you, without you obviously or blatantly doubting his ability to do so. Even if he can't bake a Pop Tart®, let him make you breakfast his way. He will be so proud, and, don't worry, if it's terrible, he will already know.

If your guy has broken your trust in a small way, the next time something similar comes up, give him the benefit of the doubt before you immediately dismiss the situation. If he cares for you, he's desperate to earn back your trust and doing this thing for you is his way of trying to do so.

Take a Risk Together

This could be anything from trying the new sushi bar down the street to going to one of those adventure camps to deciding to move your lives closer to one another.

Taking risks shows vulnerability and when you do this together, it's a great bonding experience. You now have something really big to share and you built a new level of trust in each other by sharing the experience. It's okay that you're both scared to death to cross the rope bridge—hold hands and encourage one another. It's empowering individually and as a couple! You'll never forget it!

I call these experiences "putting pennies in the jar." The pennies are great memories, and the jar is the entire collection of them. The more pennies you have, the more solid your relationship becomes.

It is like forming a mote around you and your partner that no other woman (or man) can penetrate.

Cheating will never happen.

Be Able to Give and *Receive*

All too often, one partner thinks they're giving more than they're receiving. Instead of keeping a score sheet, why not let the chips fall where they may. It's important for both partners in a solid relationship to give and receive.

There will be times when you will need him to give a little more and other times when he will need you to give a little extra. This is how relationships work. If you're constantly keeping score, quantifying someone's efforts to show love, you're missing the point.

Sometimes, you need to *let* him give. If he wants to go the extra mile for you in some way, let him. It's his way of showing his love for you. There is no balance in give and take, so just let it be what it is.

11

Questions People Ask and How to Answer Them

Many people are naturally inquisitive, and you almost hate to see them coming because you know a barrage of questions is headed your way. Still others are curious about your situation because they might be considering something similar. Your knee-jerk response to questions about your relationship might be, "It's none of your business", but what if we consider this moment one you can use to enlighten people and help them see how it *is* working?

QUESTION: Why are you in a long-distance relationship? Don't they usually fail?

This is a great question and probably the one you'll be asked most often. Your why will vary, and you don't need to go into detail because it truly *is* none of their business, but you can say something like, "Well, Josh had this great opportunity to advance his career and I didn't want him to lose that so we committed to it. And no, most long-distance relationships don't fail."

QUESTION: Do you miss having sex?
Whether you say yes or no doesn't matter here. What you want to express is that you're committed to seeing this relationship succeed and if that means less sex, you're willing to make that sacrifice for a while.

In my past LDR experience, I bet I had more sex than most of my 'together' couples!

QUESTION: Do you have phone sex?
Well, talk about nosey! The easiest and least embarrassing answer to this one is, "We manage to keep the romance alive in our own way, thanks."

QUESTION: When will you live together?
To this, you can say something like, "We have a timeframe in mind and we're hoping to be able to stick to it, barring any unforeseen circumstances. Until then, we enjoy every moment we can spend together."

QUESTION: Do you ever wonder if he's cheating on you?
This one can be a real ball-buster, but you can still manage it tactfully, "Tim and I fully trust one another. Our relationship won't work without it, and that's true whether we live in the same city or not."

Of course, I like turning things around on nosey people some-times..." Are you sure your George isn't screwing his cute secretary?"

I digress...

QUESTION: What does your family think of this?

A great answer to this might be, "I don't need the blessing of my family to have any sort of relationship, long-distance or not. If they choose to approve, that's great, but if they don't, it really doesn't impact us one way or another."

QUESTION: Isn't it expensive to have a long-distance relationship?

Without going into great detail about your finances, you can say something like, "Well, it can be, but we are very careful to plan our visits and save up gift cards and points so that we can keep the expenses to a minimum."

QUESTION: Why can't you find someone local?

Doesn't this just make you want to let out a huge sigh? How about saying, "Well, I suppose I could if I didn't have Dave, but he is very special to me, so the fact that we don't live in the same city isn't that important to me right now."

QUESTION: Are you *really* happy with this arrangement?

This is another, none-ya-business type of question, but if you're going to answer it, try this, "Yes, we're both extremely happy with our current arrangement. We choose to look at the positives of our situation and make the most of what we have together."

QUESTION: We're considering a long-distance relationship in the near future. Do you think we can do it?

This one should be easy for you, "Yes, I do think you can. Take time to do a little research and figure out if you think it will work for you. Everyone is different."

Wrapping Up

I hope you've found some valuable ways in which you can make your long-distance relationship succeed! There is no reason for failure unless someone gets bored and cheats or you don't follow the things you've read.

I'd like to summarize the eleven chapters you've just read:

- Excellent communication skills will make this relationship stronger; remember to look at situations for what's in it for your conversational partner and what their truth might be, versus yours; stay present, be understanding and manage your expectations
- Use one of the many methods described in Chapter 2 to develop and maintain a high level of intimacy with your partner—and always remember, intimacy is not sex
- Follow the Rules of Long-Distance Relationships to ensure your success

  » Have reasonable expectations

- » Use positive language when talking about your relationship
- » Remember to maintain excellent communication
- » Try to maintain a routine or schedule to facilitate talking and making plans
- » Avoid risky situations that might cause jealousy or doubt
- » Don't listen to naysayers
- » Don't make assumptions, ask
- » Stay positive
- » Limit your screen time
- » Establish boundaries and stick to them

- Plan long-distance date nights when you can't be together
- Create sexual tension
- Find ways to enjoy your time apart by having hobbies and friends you spend time with
- Recognize when things might be drawing you closer to ending your relationship and evaluate the situation
- Manage your budget to make your time together stress-free
- Build your relationship on a foundation of trust
- Know how to answer the usually rude questions people will ask in a way that won't cause you to start doubting yourself or your relationship

Author Bio

As one of Boston's top dating coaches, my books rest prominently atop the dating advice genre. In my role as a life coach, I've been known to be unorthodox, in a good way, and I break a few rules. I assist both men and women and help them understand one another.

I won't bore you with my professional bio. Instead, I will share with you the story of how I became a dating and life coach and what makes me qualified to coach you.

The irony of my story is that I come from an extremely dysfunctional family. I witnessed the marriage of my parents crumble before my eyes at an early age. Flying dishes seemed normal in my household. I came out a bit angry and I have 12 years of failed relationships to show for it.

Fortunately, I started encountering positive things in my life. I discovered that couple, that elusive, elderly couple still holding hands in the park at the ripe old age of eighty. They gave me hope. As a problem solver, I could solve anything...except relationships, damn it!

I couldn't figure out why my folks represented the norm rather than the exception to married life. Fifty-five percent of all marriages end in divorce. Why? "What's wrong?"

In 2009, after a long stretch of living the single life, I had an epiphany. I attended a Christmas show at my Dad's church. I am not a religious person, but when I saw the cheerful couples and witnessed the powerful music, I was touched. I needed answers to love and I wanted true love for myself.

I was tired of my shallow single life. I decided to study my failures and interview as many single people and couples as I could. I even watched the movie, Hitch, and it motivated me to help others.

I realized I possessed a natural ability to help others discover love, and knew it was my future. Can you guess where I started? Yep, those happy elderly couples. Sure, I got maced a few times as I approached them with questions, but the knowledge I gained was priceless!

Since then, I have met thousands of people: happy couples, unhappy couples, single people of all types, and everything in between. I quickly learned that confidence played a large role in both attracting and keeping a partner.

Men and women contact me after reading my books. I have become a "Dear Abby" of sorts. Today, after thousands of interviews, I have accomplished my goal. I broke the code and enjoy a great relationship myself. Now I plan to share my findings *with you!*

I have come to realize that even though people believe what I teach, they still suffer a serious problem. They lack the motivation and confidence to execute my tactics. A course change was required. I started concentrating on life coaching in addition to relationship coaching. If you can't love yourself, how can you love someone else? It's impossible.

Now, I concentrate on pulling people in and guiding them toward understanding themselves. I assist them in creating clarity in their lives, setting goals, and creating the path to attain those goals. I offer inspiration, passion, and spirituality with the constant live like you're dying attitude. People are transformed through my books and daily exercises.

I have written many Amazon Best Sellers, several of which reached #1 Best Seller status. Together we can build your confidence, increase your self-esteem, and propel you closer to your goals.

You will discover happiness by completing the work most people will never attempt!

Today, I travel and teach in all the sexy playgrounds: LA, South Beach, and Las Vegas. I can help you in your journey to find love and build confidence so we can transform your life.

I am not merely a best-selling author, my readers are my friends and I communicate with them di-rectly. I humbly ask you to allow me to help you. Join me on my quest for your happiness, your ex-citing journey to an extraordinary life!

Gregg Michaelsen, Confidence Builder

Get the Word Out to Your Friends

If you believe your friends would draw something valuable from this book, I'd be honored if you'd share your thoughts with them. If you feel strongly about the contributions this book made to your success, I'd be eternally grateful if you would post a review on Amazon.

You can check out all my books by going to
https://www.whoholdsthecardsnow.com/books/.

Made in United States
Orlando, FL
14 March 2022

15792481R00050